THE BLACK SHEEP

THE BLACK SHEEP

VOLUME 1

AUBRI ADGERSON

CONTENTS

PROLOGUE

Life, as we all know, is not always a fair game. Many times, the events that transcribe our lives might seem wholly nonsensical. But perhaps that's exactly how it's meant to be. Each moment unfolds for a purpose, even if it's obscured to our understanding. Have you ever felt that your struggles were nonsensical, that you were alone in this tough battle? Certainly, it's a thought that crosses the minds of many, echoing through countless generations: the perennial question of "Why?" Why me? Out of everyone who walks this earth, why must I face these trials? The truth is, the answer eludes us, but we have to cling to the notion that everything indeed happens for a reason. If you're wrestling with the belief that your life is exceptionally burdensome, let me illuminate a truth for you: you are far from alone. Countless others share their burdens with me, seeking solace or companionship through their struggles. I can't always decipher the reasons behind their confessions, but one thing is certain —there's someone holding you all in prayer. To those who've ventured into these pages, know that my thoughts and prayers ascend for you and your journeys, for each hardship may shape us, but it does not define us.

LOVE YOU ALL AND I Y'ALL IN MY PRAYERS

This book is dedicated to everyone in the struggle, everyone that is going through right now. It's ok, baby, God got you just hold on, and your reward is coming.

In loving memory of my godmother.

R.I.P Martha Lee Henley I love you, mama

To my mother: I love you, Mama, and I forgive you

To my father, I can't hate you forever.

To my right-hand chick Shauncel Brown, thank you, and I love you.

Love you all, and I ya'll are in my prayers.

ACKNOWLEDGMENTS

I would like to take a moment to express my heartfelt gratitude to God, who has always been by my side. It is through His grace that I have been blessed with the precious gift of writing, the ability to weave my thoughts into a tapestry of words that reflect my innermost feelings. Each sentence I craft is a testament to His influence in my life. In loving memory of my cherished godmother, Martna Lee Henley, may her soul find eternal peace. I feel your presence watching over me from the heavens, guiding my pen and inspiring my heart. To my beloved Granny, Shirley Bullock, my unwavering rock and pillar of strength—I cannot thank you enough for the countless lessons you imparted. You taught me the invaluable truth that I am indeed somebody special, encouraging me to embrace my individuality and to shine brightly in a world that sometimes feels dim. Your love has shaped me into the person I am today, instilling a sense of worth and purpose that I carry with me every day.

CHAPTER 1

How does a child transition from having every desire fulfilled, living a life of luxury reminiscent of the "Fresh Prince," to facing starvation, then resorting to theft, and ultimately descending into prostitution? Allow me to share my story. I was raised in what many would consider a perfect family—a father who ran his own successful business, raking in over a quarter-million dollars a year, and a mother dedicated to her work in physical therapy, earning nearly fifteen dollars an hour. I had an older brother, an older sister, and a younger brother, surrounded by the wealth and trappings that rappers glorify; we were a family that went to church, seemingly living the dream. I distinctly remember my father owning six personal cars. One day, I'd find that gleaming champagne BMW parked outside—he used to say BMW stood for 'Black Man's Wish'—next to a smaller version of the same model, then there was the classy money-green Mercedes, a sleek black Range Rover, a deep forest-green Millennium, and a sturdy Mazda Tribute ES V6. The next day might have brought a bold red Cadillac, a pristine white Mercedes, a striking blue Suburban complete with televisions and DVD players, a stylish gray Jaguar, and yet another black BMW— all shiny and new, a promise of the latest models just six months away from the next year. That's because we had money, money that was earned legally through hard work and a steadfast faith in God, living life the right way. We were never compelled to hustle, steal, or sell ourselves to acquire our possessions; they simply existed. Both my parents were preachers, with my mother possessing the gift of prophecy. My siblings and I wanted for nothing. Then, without warning, everything changed. After nearly fifteen years of sobriety, my father succumbed to drugs, embarking on an affair, feeling disillusioned by what he perceived as our family's ingratitude for his sacrifices. If only I could tell you that I thrived under this abundance. Yet, in truth, I was the black sheep, confronting the harsh reality that money cannot buy happiness, a lesson I would learn in the most painful way.

My mother spent the entire nine months of her pregnancy indulging in crack cocaine, save for a brief month when she was taken to a mental facility for her safety because she was convinced she would end my biological father's life. Can you imagine? She wandered those unforgiving streets, dragging me along on her chaotic journey to Tulip Street, clutching a can of gasoline with one hand and hiding a machete in her boot. When she first learned of my existence, panic consumed her; she attempted to throw herself from moving vehicles and recklessly down flights of stairs in desperate attempts to end it all. There were whispered conversations about getting an abortion, darkened by dread and uncertainty. When I finally made my entry into the world, I spent nearly a week in the hospital, dubbed merely "baby girl," as my mother hadn't signed the adoption papers yet, caught in a convoluted web of indecision and turmoil. But then my grandmother—oh how I adore her —and my godmother, my dear Martha Lee Henley— may she rest peacefully—intervened. My godmother strode into that sterile room, her voice steady but urgent, "Don't give her away, bring Sara home." It was at that moment they secured my place within our family, defying every chaotic whisper of my beginnings. They named me Chanel Sara Aubri' Adgerson. "Aubri'" was bestowed by my uncle Wiley "Joonie" Bullock, who thought I bore a striking resemblance to a girl he had known in Baltimore, and it just stuck with me, a badge of honor from my family. "Chanel" was inspired by my grandmother's beloved fragrance, Chanel #5, a symbol of elegance amidst our stormy lives. And "Adgerson"? That came from Kenneth Adgerson Sr., the man who believed I was his and chose to grace me with his name, a connection that remained even after the truth unfolded. When I was born, I was supposedly the most beautiful baby anyone had ever seen—a bold claim, but who was I to argue? My skin, bright red, as vivid as a sunset, embodied the Indian heritage coursing through my veins. Long, luscious dark brown hair framed my tiny face, slicked down beautifully, long enough to tie into a delicate ponytail. I was what people might call a "hairy baby," with a surprising amount of fuzz for someone just entering the world. In hushed tones, the doctors speculated about my future, suggesting I might be born mentally challenged or carry other birth defects. Yet, fate had a humorous twist in store: I was born with four nipples instead of the usual two, a quirk that faded after just a few days, leaving only the faintest reminder of its existence. As an infant, I was relatively serene, a peace that descended upon me unless hunger gnawed at my belly or my diaper demanded attention. When I hit the six-month milestone, my mother took away all my bottles and pacifiers, a swift transition that nudged me toward a newfound solace in sucking my thumb. To this day, that thumb remains my anchor, my tether to comfort, assuring me that as long as it rests between my lips, I can find a bit of contentment amidst the chaos that has defined my life.

Like many toddlers, they experience the thrilling moment of uttering their first word. But me? Well, I was an enigma, never once coaxed into the ebb and flow of conversation. I spent my days, thumb nestled in my mouth, quietly absorbing the world around me like a diligent little scientist—an observer of life's grand performance. It wasn't until the approach of my third birthday that the floodgates opened, and I began to speak, though I didn't waste time on mere fragments or simple utterances. Oh no, I launched straight into complete, full-fledged sentences as if I were composing a symphony of language from the get-go. Raised by my wise grandmother, I was never far from her gentle guidance, not even when I began my school journey. My formative years spun around her like a familiar melody, grounded in the wisdom of those who came before me —four generations, in fact—who imparted their stories and traditions long before I ever graced this Earth. The echo of the baby boomer generation, with all their dreams and struggles, shaped my very essence, preparing me for a maturity beyond my years. Yet, as a preacher's kid, my childhood was somewhat cloistered. The world seemed vast and exciting, but I found myself on the outside looking in. No Halloween treats graced my doorstep, no rebellious dances to secular music played through my speakers, no late-night escapades with friends at parties, nor the thrilling terror of scary movies punctuated my evenings. I often wonder how much richer my life might have been if those restrictions hadn't loomed large over my formative years. Alas, inevitability cast its shadow, and change was simply a part of growing up—like a tide coming in to reshape the shore.

CHAPTER 2

When I was around 11, I vividly recall a sunny afternoon, the air filled with the familiar scent of fresh haircuts and warm candy. I sat in the small, bustling foyer turned barbershop, my little brother in the chair, strands of hair cascading down around him like confetti. I had just unwrapped a piece of bright candy, the kind that dissolves slowly, and I was in stitches, laughing at my brother's animated antics in the chair. But then, without warning, the candy lodged itself in my throat, and my world turned chaotic. Instinctively, I grabbed my neck, gasping for air, while my sister cackled at my misfortune, her laughter ringing like a cruel bell, indifferent to my plight. Nobody else seemed to care; it was the routine dismissal of a child's suffering. In a desperate maneuver, I hurled myself against the cold, unyielding back of an iron kitchen chair, forcing the candy from my throat. With a violent cough, the candy rocketed across the kitchen, where it landed with a colorful splatter in the foyer, right at my brother's feet like a bizarre, fruity meteor. The nonchalant response from my family was a simple, "Oh, you really were choking," as if my brush with death was merely an awkward inconvenience. How utterly redundant. Flashback to when I was barely 2; the memories are hazy, but certain moments are etched in my mind like a neon sign. I had a penchant for swallowing oddities—a penny here, a crescent-shaped earring there, its sharp edges gleaming like danger itself. The horrifying discovery of the earring came when it finally emerged in my diaper, a stark reminder of my reckless explorations. Rushed to the hospital, I remember the sterile smell and nurses bustling about, checking to ensure I hadn't done any internal damage. I was just a toddler, curious and oblivious. Between the ages of 2 and 3, I was a bundle of chaotic energy; I recall the time I managed to put a hole in my grandmother's wall as I munched on sheetrock like it was candy. They had to drag me away from my nibbling. Little did they know that innocent consumption came with the strange gift of lead poisoning—though, fortunately, not enough to claim my life. It felt like a twisted adventure, flitting through the world with reckless abandon, surviving these near-misses like a character in some bizarre childhood saga.

It felt like the only time anyone truly noticed me was when I was in real trouble, like that one day in elementary school. I remember it vividly: I was up on the jungle gym, carefree and playful, when my foot slipped. The fall was brutal, and I can still feel the sharp sting of pain as I split myself open. That was the beginning of a long struggle, a fear that lingered into my senior year of high school; the mere thought of climbing back onto any jungle gym left me paralyzed. My right-hand chick—my twin, Celly Brown—was my rock. She encouraged me to confront my fears and gradually helped me reclaim the skies, so to speak, particularly of heights. In middle school, I threw myself into sports; I was a part of the track team at Lincolnorne Middle School. Yet even then, it seemed that everyone was too caught up in their own worlds to come watch me compete. My mother, though, she managed to squeeze in an appearance at one of my track meets. We were racing against Dunbar Middle that day, and despite missing hurdles and feeling the fatigue creep in, I finished in second place in one event and snagged first in the 100 meters. When she finally showed up, I was already weary from sprinting the 220 in someone else's stead. After the meet, my mother would tease me about how slow I was, her laughter light, but for me, it held a weight that struck deeper than she knew. I couldn't help but brush it off with a chuckle, but inside, it stung; I had given it my all while juggling multiple events without catching a breather. That week in practice, as I attempted to discipline myself for hurdles, I found my concentration slipping just like my foothold that day on the jungle gym. It was exhausting—physically and emotionally. Moments like those sometimes made me wish I had never surfaced into this world at all. Sports became a distant memory after that. The joy transformed into dread, and soon, I found myself walking away from it all, unwilling to face the field of competition again.

CHAPTER 3

For some readers, this book might feel like a bit of a marathon, full of the kind of gritty honesty that can hit hard and leave you reeling. But I can't help but bring you this unfiltered version of my journey, straight from my heart and infused with the rawness of real life. The upcoming chapters dive into some pretty crucial moments – the kind that might rattle your sensibilities. So, consider this a heads-up: parental discretion is strongly advised. We're not skimming the surface here; we're delving into the messy details, the unvarnished truths, complete with the unapologetic language and vibrant imagery that makes life what it is – intense, unrefined, and entirely true. Buckle up; it's going to be a ride filled with all the complexities of existence.

CHAPTER 4

The house we called home was, to some, a sprawling mansion filled with countless stories and memories. Its basement level boasted a fully equipped gym, inviting us to sweat and hustle, along with a spacious bathroom, ample storage, and a dedicated area where our bikes awaited the next adventure. Ascending to the second level, we found ourselves in a warm and welcoming living room, a sophisticated dining room that hosted many family gatherings, an office where dreams were penned, a cozy family room perfect for shared laughter, and yet another bathroom for our convenience, all leading to the heart of the home: the kitchen, where the aroma of countless meals mingled with heartfelt conversations. On the third level, four inviting bedrooms offered a serene escape, adorned with personal touches and memories, accompanied by a bathroom and a lovely upstairs back deck that overlooked the neighborhood, a place where we could sip our morning coffee and watch the world come alive. At the very top awaited the attic, with its nooks and crannies filled with forgotten treasures, alongside my mother's prayer room—a sanctuary of peace and reflection—plus more storage and closets bursting with the remnants of our lives. Yet, amidst all this grandeur, what stood out the most were the steps, each one a small adventure leading us through the layers of our family's tapestry, connecting the various parts of our daily lives. Outside, we had carports that shielded our vehicles and built-in decks where memories were made, conjuring a little bit of everything that defined our colorful existence.

That house, with its weathered walls and creaking floors, holds a treasure trove of memories intertwined with shadows of secrets long buried. The echoes of laughter once filled the air, but those joyful moments are now often eclipsed by the weight of untold stories. Each corner of the home whispers haunting tales, where secrets outweigh the fond recollections, transforming themselves into relentless nightmares that replay in the minds of those who dare to remember. Trauma lingers in the very fabric of the place, and pain seeps through its foundations, creating an atmosphere thick with unspoken dread.

CHAPTER 5

I have always felt an undeniable pull toward the presence of women, a magnetic force that began to awaken within me at the tender age of seven. It was during my early teenage years that I embarked on my very first relationship, a significant chapter in my young life, at the age of thirteen. My first girlfriend, a captivating girl who was eighteen at the time, entered my world with a blend of excitement and trepidation. Although our relationship was innocent—devoid of any sexual engagement—we were enveloped in the thrill of "dating." I often recall that pivotal date, October 17, 2005, etched in my memory like a cherished treasure, a symbol of youthful love and discovery. As the years whizzed by, a sense of nostalgia burgeoned within me. Fast forward to today, and I find myself standing on the precipice of our one-year anniversary—just five days away—a testament to the journey we've shared, filled with laughter, secrets, and the complexities of young love. Each moment leading up to this milestone has been a mosaic of memories, a blend of heartwarming experiences that shaped who I am today, urging me to reflect on this profound connection and the lessons learned along the way.

Thursday, October 12, 2006, was like any other day. I went to school, came home, and did my homework, not knowing the evening would bring a turn of events. I changed my school clothes and got comfortable. I had on this tan sweatsuit with these double white lines going down the side of the leg. All my chores were done, so I decided to find myself something to watch. I was sitting in the house watching the temptations on TV, and I kept hearing weights drop. So I went outside and I went outside and down the steps to the basement to see what the noise was. I saw Darryl, and I said you are down here, and so I went back upstairs. Now, Darryl was a young man my father brought to church off the streets that I had only seen twice in my life. My father had let him into the basement and didn't tell anybody. Well, about an hour went by, and I heard a knock at the door. I went to the door, and Darryl said something was wrong with the lock. So I got the key from the glass china cabinet in the dining room and went to fix the lock. When I got downstairs to the basement, I had to turn off the It"ht on the other side next to all the gym equipment. When I went to turn off the light, Darryl grabbed me and threw me on the bench press. He was grabbing my clothes, and I was yelling stop, but no one could hear me because everyone was gone, and my sister was on the third floor on the phone. He snatched my clothes off from the waist down while I kept saying no, and then all of a sudden, while holding my hands together above my head, laying his hot, sweaty, heavy, funky body on top of mine, he forced his penis into me. It was the worst pain I had ever felt in my life. When he finally got up, I ran out with my clothes all twisted. And went to sit on the porch. He rang the doorbell and asked my sister for a wet rag to wipe off the leg of his jeans where the dust from the concrete was on him from struggling with me. On top of all that, I was still a virgin before he did that, and he took the most precious thing from me: My innocence; he looked my innocence away from me. Never ever will mess with a man. Well, at least those were my intentions. That night, I laid a towel over my pillow so that my tears wouldn't stain my pillows. I cried and cried until the next morning, with a huff and sniffle here and a puff and a sniffle there. I knew I had school in the morning, but what was I supposed to do? My mother was not the warmest person to talk to. The more I cried, the more thoughts that went through my head. How? Why? Why me? I hurt. I'm bleeding… I'm not a virgin anymore…

It was Friday, October 13, 2006, I got up, but I felt so weak. We had PT, so at least I could put on some sweats. I got to school, and I felt as though the walls were closing in on me. My thoughts were tangled, and I couldn't focus at all; my mind raced with everything I was trying to suppress. I made the difficult decision to seek help and approached the guidance counselor, my heart pounding as I shared my anguish with her. The concern etched on her face told me everything I needed to know; she understood. Along with the school resource officer, they escorted me to the emergency room, where the weight of my fear felt almost unbearable. When they called my mother, I hoped for comfort but braced myself for turmoil. When she arrived, her voice escalated into a tempest of disbelief, her accusations cutting deep—she thought I was lying, that I was fabricating a tale of horror. Each word pierced through me. I couldn't comprehend how the woman who had cradled me at birth could doubt my truth. (she didn't want me. Thats how). Eventually, the detective joined us in the sterile white confines of the emergency room. My breaths became shallow as I recounted everything I could remember, down to the clothes I wore—tan sweatpants, purple penguin slippers, a simple white tee shirt, and white panties, items that had become a uniform for my pain. After my mother and the detective left to gather evidence from our home, I sat in a whirlpool of emotions, trembling between hope and despair. I had pointed out that everything would be exactly as I described it, and it confirmed what I had been saying. At last, her skepticism began to waver, yet the shadows of doubt loomed large. They pressed me with relentless questions about why I hadn't spoken to my sister about any of it. The truth lay heavy on my tongue; I was paralyzed by fear of disbelief, of hostility, of being vilified for speaking out against the very person who had wronged me. The courtroom loomed ahead, a cold, impersonal place that echoed with the murmur of justice—not always served. They offered me a way out, the option to plead the Fifth, a choice that would speak volumes; it would imply his guilt without requiring me to testify. My heart ached at the thought of having to face him again. Before the trial, he was taken for a psychiatric evaluation. When presented with questions, he feigned ignorance, acting as if he lacked even the simplest knowledge of his own life—who he was, his birthday, his age, or who his parents were. They pulled up his record, and the chilling realization struck that he had a history of similar offenses. At only seventeen, he had crossed the line of morality and safety, turning eighteen days later while appearing twice his age. Ultimately, the judgment came, and the sentence was delivered: two years for the unforgivable act he committed against me. The verdict felt painfully insufficient as if justice was slipping through my fingers like sand. I left the courtroom with a lingering sense of disbelief but a flicker of hope that one day, I might reclaim my voice and demand more than this fleeting satisfaction.

CHAPTER 6

After Darryl.was locked up, the man I had grown close to, who had taken on the role of my father figure since I was just a year old—my biological father had wanted nothing to do with me until I was nearly seven—well, my stepfather, who was a preacher, began to spread malicious gossip about me behind my back. He told my stepsister and the entire world that what happened to me wasn't real, that I had somehow 'given it up' willingly, and that I was simply afraid I might be pregnant. The weight of those words, that mischaracterization of my trauma, is something I have to carry with me for the rest of my life. Every time that conversation arises, it pierces my heart anew. Yet, curiously, he was the first to express a desire to kill the man who had wronged me. A few weeks later, I vividly remember waking in a panic at two in the morning.

Drenched in fear, I bolted down the stairs, where I stumbled upon my parents fighting. I had seen them argue before, but nothing like this. It was as if all the benevolence in their marriage had deteriorated into pure chaos—blow for blow, yelling unheard of in our home before that night. From then on, it seemed that fighting became a permanent fixture in our lives, every weekend marked by their escalating confrontations. I've never been one to handle confrontation well; it churns something uncomfortable within me. The police became a frequent, unwelcome presence at our house, so much so that I abandoned my childhood dream of becoming an officer myself.

I remember before my father left, the last struggle was out in the open. He had this sleek black convertible Mercedes Benz, a car that gleamed in the sunlight with its chrome trim and elegant lines. On that fateful day, just before he moved out, he and my mother were in another violent argument. He had to drive past the house to leave, and as fate would have it, my mother leaped over the six-foot fence, landing perfectly in the backseat as he sped around the corner. In that moment of passion and rage, she started choking him in a fit of fury, spurring him to slam on the brakes. He grabbed her by the hair, pulling her from the car with a force that made my heart race. As a child, I had thought that evening would mark the pinnacle of trauma in our family, but little did I know it was only the beginning. I nurtured a deep hatred for my father that lingered long after, a bitterness rooted in his betrayal and the pain of being talked about by the very person who was supposed to protect me. It's one thing to experience betrayal, but when it's from family, from your own parents, that anguish runs much deeper. The blend of hurt and betrayal is a raw wound, the worst kind a child should never have to endure.

CHAPTER 7

In the aftermath of everything that transpired, I found myself gravitating towards a more androgynous style, adopting boyish clothing as a shield against the world. It was a deliberate choice born from a deep insecurity, a visceral desire to obscure my true self. The weight of my experiences felt like an open secret, a palpable aura that surrounded me, making me believe everyone else was privy to my past. This overwhelming sense of exposure urged me to withdraw, to create distance from everyone except for my girlfriend, the sole anchor in an otherwise tumultuous sea of isolation. I clung to her, seeking solace in our connection, but still felt the need to cloak myself further; by dressing as a boy, I thought I could escape the unwanted gazes, the intrusive questions tethered to my history. I convinced myself that if I appeared less feminine, I could evade the spotlight that had so cruelly highlighted my pain. Part of what had happened to me stemmed from my own reluctance to attract attention, and with each piece of clothing, I donned, I was forging an armor—one that promised to protect me from further scrutiny while I navigated the labyrinth of self-acceptance.

In those turbulent times, my father made the decision to leave our home, setting into motion a series of events that would shatter our family dynamic. My mother, feeling lost and abandoned, turned deeper into the world of drugs, her dependence growing alarmingly. Nights that once felt like a child's sanctuary morphed into chaotic odysseys. She would leave the house at odd hours, often well after sunset, with her return stretching from mere hours to entire nights. As the weeks progressed, it became all too common for her to vanish for days on end, lost to whatever draw the outside world had over her. At that point, the fractures in our family led us to my older brother, who resided across town with his girlfriend and her four young children, crammed into a small, cramped space that echoed with the noise of their bustling lives. The truth, however, was that my brother and I had never seen eye-to-eye; our relationship was marred by resentment and hostility, and his disdain for me felt palpable. The house we moved into was a stark representation of their chaotic life—a cramped, grimy space where each corner seemed to harbor a different type of grime. Bugs skittered across the surfaces, the floors stuck underfoot, a testament to neglect and disarray, and an unbearable stench wafted through the air, wrapping around us like a cloak of despair. The youngest, a mere baby, wandered through this squalor, often in a diaper that had long since lost its cleanliness. Frighteningly, he was even given beer—a shocking reality for a child of only one year. Clothes lay strewn everywhere, and the place felt like a battleground of filth and disorder—far too dismal for even a reluctant recounting of specifics. Though each day blurred together, I knew I was witnessing what could only be described as a tragic decline, an unraveling tapestry of family and home that history would later come to define.

CHAPTER 8

Our time there stretched painfully over two long months, marking the end of the school year. During those weeks, I often found myself trapped in a cycle of embarrassment and desperation, with barely a change of clothes to my name. Whenever I was fortunate enough to have clean garments, it was only through the kindness of my girlfriend—she would come by, gather up my dirty laundry, and return it fresh and folded. Meanwhile, my siblings had taken to whispering harsh words, telling me that our father harbored a deep-seated hatred for me. They expressed their twisted wishes for our mother, hoping she would succumb to the streets and, in some terrible way, let her heart give out from the burden of her addictions. It was a landscape painted in anguish, one that I couldn't bear. As the days dwindled, the hunger gnawed at me. Lunchtime became a beacon of hope, and I would devour everything in sight, each bite a reminder of the scarcity that awaited me later. My brothers and sisters—a pack consumed by their own struggles—offered me no solace or nourishment, and thus, I often went hungry. The summer stretched on endlessly, unraveling into almost two entire months devoid of food after school let out. The only occasions I ate were when my girlfriend, with her genuine care, brought me meals, a lifesaver in a sea of neglect. My family was too preoccupied with the plight of their own life and other things, particularly my little brother, who struggled with diabetes, to even spare thought for my well-being. Left to fend for myself, I was haunted by those moments of emptiness, both in my stomach and in my heart. The choice of where to turn was painful; my oldest sister wouldn't open her home to me because of the accusations of her husband's unwanted advances toward me. It seemed futile to think she would believe the truth of my innocence. Still, I held out hope for her. My prayers for her well-being were sincere, for I knew that when the shadows of our lives finally came to light, she would face a heart-wrenching reality.

Well, it reached a point of desperation, a moment where my instincts kicked in, and I found myself stealing money from my own brother so that I could put food in my stomach. It was a grim decision, but in that harsh reality, I had to do what was necessary. It was truly a matter of survival, the fittest versus the rest, and I desperately needed to prove that I could thrive without their support. As the dust of that chaotic period settled, slowly but surely, all eleven of us found our way back to my house. It was a makeshift refuge, but there was a glaring absence; my mother had vanished, leaving behind unanswered questions, while my father was lost somewhere in his own world, likely holed up in his own space, oblivious to the turmoil around us. They attempted to transform my humble abode into a replica of the chaos that was the other house, but I stood my ground, refusing to let the disorder spread further. At just fourteen, I became the reluctant caretaker, tirelessly cleaning up after adults who should have known better. All they wanted was to indulge in their drinks and revel in their parties while I was left to navigate the role of babysitter, caught in a whirlwind of responsibilities that felt far too heavy for my young shoulders.

I can vividly recall one sweltering afternoon when I wandered into the kitchen. There, in hushed tones, I overheard my brother and sister plotting their next move, a sinister plan to send my mother behind bars. It all stemmed from a night of chaos, a confrontation between her and my sister that spiraled so out of control that legal action was taken. They left for court, and it felt like barely twenty minutes passed before they burst back through the door, exuding a triumphant glee as if they'd just won a foul lottery. "Chanel, guess what? Your mama's locked up!" My brother crowed, his voice dripping with malice. "I hope they give that crackhead life—wouldn't mind if someone took her out in there." Those were the cruel words I had to endure, venomous whispers that cut me deeply, reminding me of the fractured world we navigated together. Hearing such things gnawed at my insides. What could I do but swallow hard and remain silent, the weight of their feelings pressing down like an anchor? When the inevitable came, and my mother was incarcerated, Uncle Wiley emerged like a beacon of hope, sweeping me away from the debris of our family drama. He took me in, wrapping me in a shield of unyielding kindness during the dark months that followed. Every visiting day, he would take me to see her, his solemn expression a reminder of the normalcy we had lost. Uncle Wiley kept me well-fed, ensuring I had meals that were more than just survival rations, and he treated me to shopping trips that filled my closet with new clothes, offering a semblance of joy amid the turmoil. I began to believe that perhaps God was looking out for me, steering me away from despair and into the hands of love. That light, that flicker of compassion, is what keeps me pushing forward—my resolve firm, for I hold onto the belief that something extraordinary awaits me just around the corner.

Not long after, my mother was back in court, this time needing to enter rehab for her drug problems. Sundays became a sacred day for me; I committed to being there, no matter what. My little brother and sister would tag along occasionally, but it was mostly my girlfriend who ensured I made it each week. No matter the weather—whether it was rain, hail, sleet, or snow—I showed up. Church was my anchor, too; I never missed a service, knowing that was where my strength was rooted. Hearing my mother's voice on the phone twisted my heart with pain; the hurt in her tone was palpable. Seeing her trapped behind those four walls, unable to break free, was pure torment for me. I felt it deep in my bones. When she finally returned home, a wave of relief washed over me like a long-awaited dawn.

My mama came home and was there for about a month, until one day…

CHAPTER 9

The company you keep can either lift you up or drag you down, shaping your choices in ways you never imagined. It's a lesson that hit my mother hard. For a while after finishing rehab, she seemed alright, like she was on the mend. But soon, I caught glimpses of those old, familiar signs creeping back into her life, and it shattered me. Seeing her struggle to resist those old temptations felt like someone was squeezing my heart into a vice. The powerlessness to pull her back weighed on my spirit like a stone lodged deep inside. As the chaos of my own life began to spiral, those moments of agony became all-consuming. I found myself retreating into whispers of prayer and tears that fell like rainstorms. The pain of hugging my mama through the cold bars of a jail cell or the stark walls of rehab haunted me. It felt crucial, almost life-or-death, to connect with her during those moments of heartache. I knew every fiber of my being screamed against the thought of reliving that nightmare again, of watching her slip through my fingers once more.

As the days stretched into months, the grip of her addiction tightened around us, constricting like a vice. It became increasingly difficult to keep up with our mounting bills, a never-ending avalanche of overdue notices and final demands. Everything was spiraling downward, the horizon darkening with each passing moment. At that time, I was trapped in a stagnant existence, unable to secure a job or contribute anything meaningful. My girlfriend, burdened yet determined, tried to be my lifeline. She would drive me to various places in a desperate attempt to earn a little money; there was one instance where I pushed my limits and ventured farther than I had ever dared before. It was a reckless journey—one I soon vowed never to repeat. Despite the meager dollars I managed to scrape together, I prioritized my little brother's needs above all else. His condition as a diabetic meant daily meals and consistent access to medication were not merely preferences but essentials that kept him alive. Each dollar I earned was a brick laid in the fragile foundation of our survival, a shield against the overwhelming chaos of helplessness that threatened to consume us all.

There was a moment etched in my memory when my younger brother fell ill, and his father, who had promised to come and fetch him, never appeared. In that instant, the realization struck me hard: it wasn't just our mother who carried the burden of disappointment and absence. My brother suffered greatly, his small body wracked with vomiting. In a panic, I tried to reach out to anyone who might help, but the calls went unanswered, leaving me feeling helpless. Determined to do whatever I could, I took the little money I had set aside for his meals the next day and made my way to the store, my heart heavy with worry. I returned with a bottle of ginger ale, some Pepto-Bismol, and a handful of other remedies I hoped would soothe him. When I walked back through the door, a wave of dread washed over me at the sight of him: face down in the toilet, the image of vulnerability and suffering. I rushed to his side, and as he lifted his head, he grasped my hand with a weak yet fervent grip. Looking deep into my eyes, he uttered words that felt like a lifeline to my soul: "I thought I didn't have anybody, but I know that you got me no matter what." At that moment, a warmth spread through me; I felt as though I had finally done some-thing right in a world that often felt chaotic and unfor-giving. The connection between us deepened, and I came to understand that sometimes, it is in our darkest hours that we truly find out who we are meant to be for one another. It was a lesson in love, resilience, and the unbreakable bond of family.

At the tender age of fifteen, I took my first steps into the world of work, a sweet liberation from the confines of youth. Four elder men, seasoned hands weathered by years of toil, were dismantling the carports that stood like gentle giants in my backyard. Curious, I ventured outside, my pajamas still a soft embrace about me, and to my own astonishment, I found a rhythm among their labors, a dance I led with youthful vigor, outpacing them with ease. When their boss returned, the spark of surprise ignited in his eyes mirrored my own triumph. He offered me a gateway job at the local carwash, a place where suds would become my trade and coins would jingle in my pocket. The pay was modest, but each bill I tucked away as a secret gift brought me closer to survival, painting dreams brighter than the stars. As days danced on, a shift in my fortunes came—the owner's wife, with her gracious smile, entrusted me with the tasks of her household, her hands guiding me not just in chores but in camaraderie, and her pay was indeed a generous treasure. Months flew by like leaves in the autumn breeze until the winds whispered caution. A man joined their ranks, shadowed with intentions far too dark, seeking the innocence of girls too young. He approached me, eyes slick with something I knew I must resist. But oh, how close he came to taste the fury of my defiance; a tension thick as smoke hung between us, a heartbeat away from catastrophe. I stood my ground, unyielding, for in that moment, I was not just a girl in pajamas—I was a storm ready to unleash its strength.

CHAPTER 10

For my sweet sixteen birthday, I received a vibrant "Sweet 16" balloon that danced playfully in the air, a heartfelt card filled with well-wishes, and a comforting stuffed animal—a gift from a kind woman who lived across the street and was friends with my mother. Strangely, my mother was absent from the day's celebrations. Seeking a sense of freedom and the warmth of companionship, I spent my days on my girlfriend's college campus, navigating the bustling environment of her life, immersing myself in studies and laughter. It was here, surrounded by youthful dreams and academic pursuits, that I found solace. But just as I was finding my footing, my mother, in a moment of panic or perhaps misunderstanding, called the police, insisting that I had run away. I hadn't fled; I was merely taking a brief vacation from the storm of confusion that surrounded me, attending school daily, punctual and passing—hardly the mark of a runaway. When my mother finally arrived in her newly repaired car, she brought not just a sense of urgency but a whirlwind of change. She announced we were moving, and our lives would soon be confined to the limit of a storage unit as we placed our belongings away. The tidbits of my life, the memories and items that tethered me to my past, were reduced to material remnants, a reflection of our fleeting existence. We moved in with my uncle, navigating a season of uncertainty, yet amidst the chaos, we rekindled our connection to faith, rediscovering the solace of church. In this new chapter, I found an unexpected opportunity to travel with the dance team—a vibrant escape that carried me to the vibrant streets of Atlanta, where I performed and twirled beneath the bright city lights. It was an exhilarating experience, yet like a fleeting dream, it felt ephemeral, highlighting how quickly the precious moments of life can slip away.

At seventeen, standing on the threshold of adulthood as a high school senior, I often find myself overwhelmed by the tangled web of my circumstances. College is on the horizon, a glimmer of hope promising a brighter future, yet the streets still call to me like a siren in the dark, tempting and familiar. I can't help but feel that there's more to life than this constant fight for survival in a world filled with shadows. Living with my mother, there's an uncomfortable distance that weighs heavily in the air, an unspoken truth that we coexist but don't connect. It stings—this reverberating ache of isolation—that despite sharing the same roof, I rarely get to see or talk to her. The moments we could share slipped away like sand through my fingers, leaving me with a haunting sense of loss and yearning. I often find myself pacing late at night, trapped in a battle with my thoughts. Who do I truly blame for the mess our lives have become? I've shouldered the weight of guilt for too long, feeling like I am somehow responsible for everything that has turned sour. My father, locked behind bars, feels like a ghost in my life—an absence that echoes with unanswered questions. Some days, I wonder how different things might have been if I had never drawn breath in this world. If I hadn't been subjected to the horrors of trauma—if that dark chapter hadn't unfolded—would the spiral into substance abuse have ever begun? The thought is suffocating. I yearn to extend my hand and lift my family from this pit of despair, yet I remain hopelessly stuck, unprepared to be the savior I dream of. Every prayer I whisper carries the weight of my ambitions—to someday emerge from this chaos and pull us toward light. One day, I remind myself, I'll be strong enough to mend the frayed threads of my family's bond and help weave us back together.

CHAPTER 11

My life is a tapestry woven from simple threads, each one telling a story of resilience and determination. I'm not someone who enjoys drama or chaos; rather, I see my existence as a raw and unfiltered version of survival of the fittest. In this world, if I don't take action, no one else will, and that realization drives me daily. My hands are my most trusted tools; working with them brings me joy and purpose. Dreams fuel my ambition, and I envision a future where I'm a talented mechanic, churning out repairs and transformations in a garage of my own. Eventually, I aspire to expand my horizons by launching my own construction business, building not only structures but dreams for others as well. As I navigate my senior year of high school, I'm filled with hope, striving to earn that diploma, which represents not just an achievement but a ticket out of the struggles that have marked my teenage days. But life isn't without its hurdles. The weight of my financial situation presses down hard, with the economy leaving me jobless—each day a reminder of the challenge it poses. My relationship with my mother is mired in uncertainty; despite my efforts to believe there's hope for her recovery, I can't shake the nagging feeling that she may still be entangled with her past, haunted by the same demons that were present two years ago. The sight of familiar symptoms grieves me deeply, pulling at my heartstrings, a constant reminder of fragility and loss. To escape the turmoil and keep my thoughts in order, I turned to writing—a passion that ignited within me at an early age. By the time I was eight, I had crafted my first story, a testament to my imagination. Now, I'm diligently working on a new book titled "Live Life to the Fullest." Within its pages lies a collection of my thoughts, reflections, and aspirations—words that shine brightly against the shadows surrounding me. Each sentence I pen brings me solace, a reminder that I can create my own path amidst the chaos.

When I spill my soul onto the page, I weave together whispers, echoes of conversations shared, threads of truth that flutter like dreams in the wind. It may seem just a casual utterance, a spoken phrase, but oh, to me, it embodies life itself—a vivid tapestry of emotions, rich and vibrant. I think back to the days of yore when R. Kelly dared to dream he could soar like an eagle, and it catches me off guard. Never in a million fleeting seconds did I envision that my journey would unfold like a tempestuous novel, each chapter a wild adventure. Yet, with a heart full of gratitude, I bow my head to the heavens and give thanks for every heartbeat; I bestow upon Him the fullest praise. I don't share my truth for the sake of recognition or applause, not for strangers to claim they know my name, but to throw a lifeline to others who might feel lost, to uplift those wandering in shadows—this, my testimony, stitched together by the fabric of family ties, the trials of education, and the bonds of camaraderie. Each path I tread can pull me taut with tension; which of these wells of connection weighs down the heart most heavily? But through it all, I cling to my music, crafting verses that dance with authenticity, each line infused with the pulse of real life, nothing invented or fabricated within this sanctuary. I entwine a rhythm around my narrative and let it slide delicately into your ears like a soft serenade. They may call me peculiar; they may label me eccentric, yet I stride ever-forward, eyes fixed on the horizon, my back straight against the burden of doubt. Many may not grasp the essence of who I am the intricacies of my spirit, but I remain unwavering, steadfast in my essence regardless of the names that fall from lips like leaves in autumn. What matters most is the answer I whisper back to the world. I shall not allow their negativity to anchor me in despair; instead, I let it fuel my resolve, sculpting joy from the challenges that attempt to dim my shine.

MARCH 17, 2009

TRU STORY

I sag my pants low, just shy of my knees.
My t-shirt boasts words, sharp as a breeze.
If I shared my saga, every joy and strife
Would that twist your view of my life?
Maybe I'll trade for stiff Dickies, tailored just right,
Ironed, creased, in black,
No less bright. A crisp button-up to redefine my attack,
While shiny black shoes sit polished in the back, is it the
flair of my fashion that causes the riff?
Or the tales I tell, what's real, what's myth?
But no matter the change, without a pause or a sigh,
I'm still a masterpiece, a star in the sky.

In the attire of life's grand parade,
You must don a visage that doesn't fade.
Men, it's not mere suits that define your grace,
Consider khaki pants, a collared embrace, And rugged
Timberlands, ready to pace.
Ladies, let modesty grace your attire,
Too much allure can set hearts afire,
With whispers of sin that tempt as they linger, Know the
power wrapped in each finger.
Embrace soft denim, let comfort be found,
Allowing your spirit to roam unbound.
This dress code reflects the journey we tread,
Your shirt, the fine moments that swirl in your head,
Your pants, the skirmishes faced every day,
While shoes lead to terrains yet to play.
How many victories can you claim,

When the burden of strife weighs down your name?
To fight, we need hands, both sturdy and true,
Exploring the world with love as our cue.
Cover your heart when you lift it in praise,
And walk new paths through life's tangled maze.
In boldness, I fashion resilience, I soar,
For the footprints I make, no one can ignore.

MARCH 18, 2009
THE WORST REJECTION

You catch a glimpse of your life lurking just behind your
eyes,
A flicker of memories, a collage of fleeting goodbyes.
But then, like a thief in the night, you suddenly feel the
chill,
A heavy shroud descends, and your heart knows its still.
Silence wraps around you, a curtain drawn tight,
Yet, in that hushed abyss, a voice pierces the night.
"Welcome, dear wanderer, to my unyielding domain,
But alas, you're not welcome here; leave your sin and
disdain."
"Is that you, God? Is it true?" you tremble within,
Desperate for mercy but lost in the din.
"I am not your savior, nor your friend wrapped in blue,
I see your tangled choices, the poison that flowed
through."

With every word spoken, the air thickens with dread,
A man with a gaze like iron stands, whispering what's
said.
"Flee from this shadow, for there's no room for your
kind,
What would you feel should the Creator deny your
mind?"
Times you thought redemption was just a breath away,
Insistent, you'd muster the strength to turn from
dismay.
You never expected that the final dust would settle, but
here, at this moment, life's reset on the petal.
How do we reach the hearts held fast in sin's embrace?
To tell them of the fleeting nature, the tragedy of grace?
For your reckless nights may vanish with the dawn,
And in a heartbeat, all you cherished could be gone.
In this undying darkness you face, you cry,
Asking for a chance when you never had to try.

On the path toward redemption,
the first stride is deep repentance.
"How much longer?" you'll query as the clock ticks by,
Before you inhale your final breath, your last desperate
sigh.
Daily, we're the judges, our own verdicts unfurled,
So, reconsider before casting stones in this world.
When that reckoning day arrives, and He's on high,
You'll be shown all your misdeeds, the hidden, the sly.
Will you be cast aside or welcomed with grace,
To join the celestial choir, basking in space?
Even in those old scriptures, Jesus let tears flow,
You'll be freed from your sorrows every pain you ever
know.
Life is what you fashion it, a canvas to define,

Yet here you linger, worrying about my line. So before
you embark on that long, somber ride,
Get your life in order; do not let it slide.
And are you certain to be seen,
When you face the judgment from the King serene?

The skin I wear tells a story profound,
Does that make me different, set apart from the crowd?
Because I am African American, wrapped in this hue,
Does it label me with burdens, a life misconstrued?
Must I walk in shadows, the offspring of the unwise,
Doomed to echo the doubts that whisper in lies?
Just because I dance to a beat not your own,
Does that render me lazy, stripped of my throne?
Does the way I dress, with a swagger you disdain,
Diminish my worth, yet I rise through the pain?
Can I not be a lady in the skin of a thug,
Spreading love like a flower, sharing compassion like
a hug?
But in this weary world, where kindness is rare,
Where do I find the love that can lift me in prayer?
To forge ahead and thrive, in well-being to dwell,

Even when faces turn cold, like a storm in a shell.
I long to whisper my dreams into the night's gentle air,
To keep singing my song, with hope woven with care,
For I understand my journey, with all its twists and
turns,
In the glow of my spirit, a fire forever burns.

y writing emerges as a profoundly intimate outlet, a sanctuary where the myriad wounds I harbor can find expression and solace. Each word I carefully inscribe acts as a stepping stone on my path of healing, a living testament to the trials I've weathered and the burdens I've carried along the way. But this narrative extends beyond the bounds of my own experience—it's a lifeline I throw to others navigating the turbulent waters of life, gently reminding them that even amidst the fiercest storms, there lies a possibility to chart a course toward tranquility. The reality of life is indeed formidable; it hurls unexpected challenges that can feel immensely unjust. Yet, let's take a moment to confront the truth—aren't we all united in this intricate tapestry of existence? Your story, like your unique fingerprint, constitutes an irreplaceable facet of who you are. Just as no two lives are inscribed with the same experiences, even twins who share the same womb bring forth entirely distinct personalities, along with their own singular imprints that distinguish them. Each personal narrative forms a magnificent tapestry intricately woven from the threads of our struggles, victories, and the rich spectrum of emotions we encounter along life's journey. When we fully embrace our stories, we not only validate our pain but also pay homage to the unwavering resilience that propels us forward, fostering connections that unite us allowing for deeper understanding and compassion to flourish within our families and communities. In this shared journey of healing and growth, we find the courage to uplift one another, recognizing that every voice matters and every story holds a piece of the greater mosaic of humanity.

APRIL 24, 2009
THE LOST FEELING

In this vast and bitter world, you find yourself a solitary figure perched upon the precipice of despair. The climate around you is as chill as the disdain of a thousand absent friends and family, for in this cruel expanse, a comforting presence is but a whisper in the wind. Your heart, a fragile vessel, bears the insurmountable weight of sorrow—a profound ache that gnaws at your very being, leading you to ponder the worth of existence itself. The wellspring of emotion, long dammed behind the eyes, threatens to overflow in a torrent of tears, and in that fateful moment, as if pulled by an unseen hand, the deluge breaks forth, and you find yourself consumed by the tempest of grief.

OCTOBER 17, 2009

THAT LOVE

In the depths of the heart, there lies an unexplainable love, a tender tether that binds souls when they draw near. It's a love that weathers the passing years, embracing every shade of existence—the joyous days singing in harmony and the stormy nights echoing with sorrow. It is the whispered comfort in tears, the warm embrace that fills the void, holding you close as if the world outside has paused, as if time itself holds its breath in reverence of your union. This love is a steadfast guardian, present in the light of day and the silence of night, a lantern that flickers yet never fades. It dances in the rain, cloaking you in its gentle embrace, shielding you against the chill of despair and pain. Together, we forge a bond, an unyielding promise that drifts on the wings of hope, whispering that what we cherish will remain anchored in our hearts. In craving and yearning, we offer our all, pouring out our souls even when the ground beneath trembles with uncertainty. Our love becomes a symphony of sharing and caring, a serenade that carries us through life's shifting tides. This love, our guiding star, is a flight of dreams that propels us upwards; the sky becomes merely a canvas, for our love reaches beyond the clouds to touch the very essence of infinity. Like grasping a soft, serene dove, gently cradling its fragile form in the palm of your hand, this love uplifts, gifting us wings. In its embrace, we find freedom—an exhilarating sense that existence is undeniably sweeter, that we can soar above, and it doesn't get any better than this.

THIS IS ONLY THE BEGINNING.